Natalia—
A beautiful
rose!

The Little Rose

Washam

THE LITTLE ROSE
By Sheri Fink

FIRST EDITION

Many things grow in the garden
that were never sown there.

~Thomas Fuller, Gnomologia, 1732

There once was a Little Rose that grew amid a bed of flourishing weeds on the side of the road. The Little Rose didn't quite fit in and never understood why the other plants treated her differently. She looked up to the other plants around her and admired them. She hoped that she could be just like them when she grew up.

Everything was fine until the Little Rose got her first bloom, then some of the other plants started treating her very badly, making fun of her and talking and whispering behind her back. Soon, all of the other plants acted as if she was undesirable, even though she never did anything to deserve it.

The Little Rose would cry and cry because she couldn't understand why they were acting that way or what she had done to upset them. She tried to make things better by being extra nice to all of the other plants. But, no matter how hard she tried, the other plants continued to treat her like she didn't belong…and she was beginning to feel that way, too.

Disappointed and confused, she kept to herself and hoped the other plants would just ignore her and leave her alone. The Little Rose was very sad and lonely and wanted desperately to make things better or get away, but she couldn't. After all, she thought she was getting the basics she needed: a little water when it rained, and some occasional sunshine when it wasn't blocked by the other plants. And, her roots were buried in the soil, so how could she ever leave? And, besides, where could she go even if she could get away?

So, she resigned herself to try to make the best of the situation and became part of the background. The Little Rose's leaves stayed small and she didn't bloom anymore. If a bud miraculously appeared, she would use her thorns to cut it off before any of the other plants noticed.

One morning, she noticed a new bud had appeared overnight. This time, the Little Rose carefully examined the bud and wondered what it would look like if she allowed it to grow. Just then, she noticed that a Lady was walking by. The Lady spotted the Little Rose's bloom and wondered aloud, "what are you doing here?" The Little Rose was afraid and thought that maybe the Lady could see that she just didn't belong. Sadness washed over her as the Lady touched her leaves. The Little Rose stood perfectly still and felt ashamed.

When the Lady left, the other plants made fun of her and said that even humans could see how ugly and worthless she was. The Little Rose cried. Deep down, she was starting to believe them.

The Lady returned the next day. This time, she had some tools the Little Rose had never seen before. The Lady placed a tool into the ground next to the Little Rose and began digging a circle all around her. The Little Rose was scared and thought that the Lady was getting rid of her. Although she was terribly afraid of what was next, part of her was relieved to be leaving the unhappy bed where she had been misunderstood and mistreated.

The Lady carefully tucked the Little Rose into a bucket with some soil and carried her away with her, away from all the hurt and pain, and everything the Little Rose ever knew.

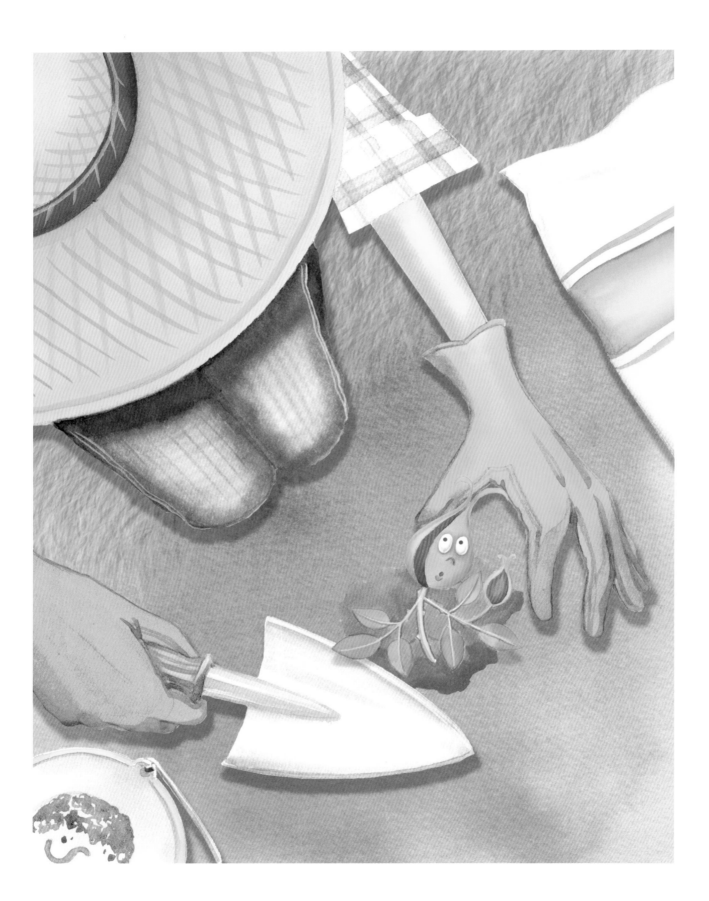

After a short walk, the Lady stopped and set the bucket down. The Little Rose didn't know what to expect next. The Lady lifted her out of the bucket and gently placed her into a hole in the ground. The Lady swept soil over her roots and surrounded her with mulch. She then gave the Little Rose a luxurious bath of fresh water and plant food, something she had never experienced before. "Just perfect," the Lady said with a smile.

When the Lady went inside, the Little Rose opened her eyes and saw that she was in the front row of a flowerbed in the Lady's front yard. She wasn't crowded in like she had been previously. In fact, she had a delightful spot right in the afternoon sunshine with plenty of room to stretch out and grow.

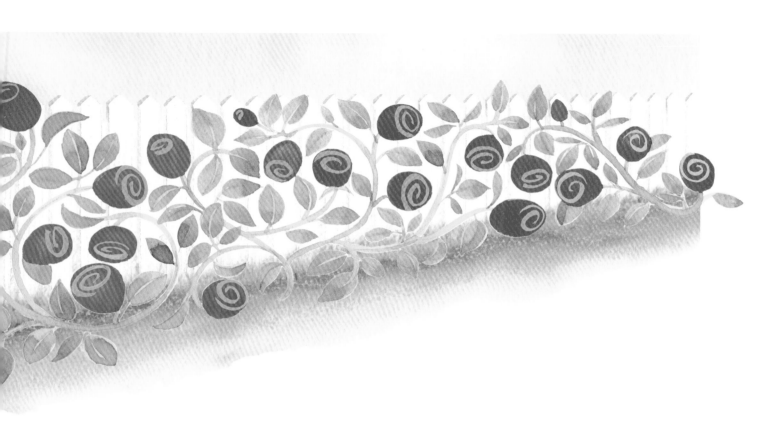

As she took in her new surroundings, the Little
Rose realized that she wasn't alone. The flowerbed had
many inhabitants, all gorgeous roses. They were all much
larger and taller than the Little Rose. At first, she was
intimidated by their beauty. She had never seen plants
like these before. Their colors were so rich and they had
blooms just like hers, only much larger and more vibrant.

Just as the Little Rose began to wonder about how she would fit in, the other roses began doting on her. They thought she was beautiful and were happy to have her in their flowerbed. The roses spent their days admiring the sunshine and befriending butterflies and birds. They were much too busy enjoying life and feeling gratitude to criticize and compete with each other. The Lady checked on the Little Rose daily and made sure that no weeds were allowed to crowd out her beauty.

The Little Rose, content at last, grew and flourished in her new environment. Never again did she try to hide who she was. She came to understand that she had always been very special and that just because the plants around her didn't see it, that didn't make it untrue. Well cared for and surrounded with love, the Little Rose experienced true joy. She grew more and more beautiful every year and lived happily ever after.

Just like the Little Rose, you are unique, special, and beautiful. Seek friends who appreciate you for who you really are and encourage you to be your best; it is in those environments where you will truly bloom and grow.